HEROIC EMBLEMS

HEROIC EMBLEMS

IAN HAMILTON FINLAY
AND RON COSTLEY

INTRODUCTION
AND COMMENTARIES
BY STEPHEN BANN

Z PRESS
CALAIS · VERMONT
1977

LIBRARY OF CONGRESS CATALOG CARD NUMBER: 77–87812
ISBN: 0–915990–10–5

The publication of this book was made possible by a
grant from the National Endowment for the Arts
in Washington, D.C., a Federal Agency.

Z Press Publications are edited by Kenward Elmslie

PRINTED IN USA

CONTENTS

INTRODUCTION

In the opening chapter of his *Studies in Seventeenth-Century Imagery*, Mario Praz puts the question: 'And above all, are emblems really such dead things?' The point of his exhaustive historical and bibliographical study is, of course, to answer this question with a resounding negative. Emblems are not merely curiosities and aberrations of a bygone age, collected on the same superficial basis as stamps or cigarette-cards. They are an integral aspect of the sensibility of the century which gave them such prominence, and, what is more, their tradition can still be identified, in a lightly disguised form, in combinations of text and image which are employed up to the present day. Praz's plea for the serious study of emblems has not gone without a hearing. Three years after the publication of the second, 'considerably increased' edition of his *Studies*, Arthur Henkel and Albrecht Schöne brought out their monumental collection, *Emblemata*. Armed with these two superb reference works, the student of emblems would no longer have to spend his time searching through 'second-hand booksellers' catalogues': he could take it for granted that his area of study was respectable, that is would no longer provoke 'the same expression of unconcern' as 'Americana [sic], Erotica, or Occultism'.

Despite the apparent good faith of Praz's plea, it remains difficult to take his justification of the emblem at its face value. In the first place, the example which he gives of the continuing vitality of the emblem tradition—'stamps issued for the tenth anniversary of the Fascist regime'—is scarcely such as to arouse and stimulate the intelligence. In the second place, and on a much more important level, Praz makes a significant admission where he refers to emblems as 'literature'. This suggests not only the fairly obvious point that our access to the emblems of the period is through the collected 'emblem books', but also the implicit assumption that they stand apart from the general development of representational systems in post-Renaissance painting. Yet a treatise like Cesare Ripa's *Iconologia* is not only an exercise in the interpretation of emblems: it also provides, through the formula that 'an image is a definition', a crucial stage in the scientific study of representation (Hubert Damisch has noted the fact, while pointing out the virtual absence of references to Ripa in Praz's study). In his fascinating essay 'Icones Symbolicae', E. H. Gombrich has further underlined the centrality of the emblem. For him it is far from being a literary genre, or a genus apart, standing as it does in the main line of development from the postulates of Platonic and Aristotelian aesthetics. Indeed Gombrich describes the emblem as a privileged means of revealing 'an aspect of the structure of the world' which is therefore worthy of serious philosophical attention.

We have come a long way from the celebratory Fascist stamps. But of course, the validity of the emblem in a particular historical context does not warrant our taking it seriously in the connection of contemporary art and imagery. In the English-speaking world, particularly, we have to correct for a development of the emblem which has withdrawn it progressively from mature consideration. John Bunyan no doubt began the rot, with his collection of *Divine Emblems* specifically for the use of children. If Bunyan reduced the emblem's role to the banal illustration of insipid moral texts, Robert Louis Stevenson reacted against his sanctimonious tone two centuries later by publishing his delightfully satirical *Moral Emblems* with his young step-son, Lloyd Osbourne. But both collections belong within the curious economy of British culture, which tends to relegate to the province of humour or children's reading all those forms which violate the taboo between visual and verbal matter. The raising of this taboo is surely long overdue.

We therefore have, on the one hand, a strong justification for further study of the emblem in its historical and aesthetic context, and on the other a balance to redress in considering the art of our own day. The fact that Gombrich stops just short of making the contemporary review which his studies point towards need not on the whole disconcert us. In the circumstances it is, after all, our opportunity to take up the challenge as readers of the present collection of emblems. For Finlay does not simply take as a neutral 'medium' the emblem or *impresa*—a unified combination of image and text (or motto), such as might have appeared in the emblem books of the seventeenth century. He mobilises the gap between the modern period and that of the Renaissance, just as the emblematists themselves signified the gap between their own period and the Graeco-Roman world through the choice of classical tags and quotations. He sets before us a cultural tissue in which these various levels—the Classical, the Renaissance and the Modern—are indissolubly linked.

Yet Finlay is not solely concerned with the layering of symbolic and emblematic themes. The whole collection is animated and unified by the notion of modern heroism, made concrete by the allusions to land, air and sea warfare in the present century. For a man of the seventeenth century like Thomas Blount, who translated Henry Estienne's *Art of Making Devises* into English, the emblem also had a special connection with modern heroism. He underlined the point by supplementing his translation with 'a catalogue of Coronet-Devises both on the King's and Parliament's side, in the late Warres'. Finlay shows the same lack of partiality in the citations which he makes from the weaponry of two World Wars and the Nuclear Age.

One may suppose that a more general, and profound, point is being made here about the tradition of Western culture as a whole. In his *Map of Misreading*, Harold Bloom recalls Ernst Robert Curtius' studies on the classical tradition and underlines his view that this tradition 'could be apprehended clearly "only" for the twenty-five centuries from Homer to Goethe'. Homer, Bloom reminds us, is still the inevitable precursor even 'if you happen to agree with William Blake when he cries aloud that it is Homer and Virgil, the Classics, and not the Goths and Vandals that fill Europe with wars'. Homer, though he is not in fact named in any of the stated references, is indeed the inevitable precursor for this collection of emblems. Yet, having followed the argument thus far, we are obliged to pursue it. In the centuries which follow Goethe, the Romantic and Modern epochs, we are maintained (so Bloom suggests) in our sense of that Homeric prototype through awareness of our own 'belatedness'. Perhaps Ian Hamilton Finlay's emblems, as indeed much of his recent work, can be seen as a strategy for belatedness. We rise to the clear vision of our cultural state as the codes of the past range before our view.

HEROIC EMBLEMS

Among the favourite subjects for the original *imprese* were the various machines of contemporary warfare: siege-engines, flint-lock guns and numerous types of cannon. Here is a modern equivalent for these citations from the technology of war. But the motto which is added casts the device back into an entirely classical context. The three words employed, which are a fragment of the work of the pre-Socratic philosopher Heraclitus, imply that the tank's 'fire-power' holds two symbolic meanings: as an index of its dominant role in modern field warfare, and also as a metaphor of fire as the governing principle of the universe. The tank is the modern equivalent of Heraclitus' thunderbolt, in that it represents not only the supreme natural force of destruction, but also the dynamic element which regulates the cosmos.

It may be added that this fragment from Heraclitus has attracted numerous different interpretations. Part of its ambiguity lies in the fact that the 'thunderbolt' is both a conventional personification of Zeus by synecdoche (substitution of the part for the whole) and a metaphor illustrating the philosopher's own cosmology. The new *impresa* retains and builds upon this ambiguity. The tank's equivocal status suggests a conjuncture of traditional Epic form, in which the divine guarantee of order is always present, and the demythologised forms of Modernism.

The motto employed here has an almost legendary origin. The Roman Emperor Vespasian took as his device a dolphin wrapped around an anchor, with the text 'Propera tarde' indicating the meaning above in a different verbal form. Aldus Manutius, the Renaissance typographer who invented italic type, also chose the emblem of the dolphin and anchor, supplementing the definition of imperial policy with his own warning of the necessary delays of the printing industry. There is moreover the popular proverb 'More haste, less speed', which places the oxymoron on a general, prudential level already anticipated in the 'moral' conclusion to Aesop's fable of the Hare and the Tortoise. If the value of a motto lies, as Gombrich suggests, in 'its capacity to be generalised', then this simple binary opposition in its many transformations achieves a kind of exemplary significance.

The device of the flail tank as the 'body' of this motto breaks, however, with preceding usage. There is a covert reference to the emblem books in the naming of the tank which, as a 'Sherman Crab', recalls the frequent and felicitous use of the crab in *imprese*. The associations of slow and circumspect behaviour which we lend to the crab here serve as a complement to the motif of the flail-chains, whose purpose is to explode any buried mines in advance of the tank's passage. Further commentary on this witty 'updating' of a traditional figure and motto might concentrate upon the motif of the flail-chains—is self-discipline (scourging) the pre-requisite for a safe passage through the 'minefield' of life?

Once again, it is a question of 'translating'—through hyperbole—the form of a pre-existing type of emblem. Here the reference is not to the traditional store of moral precepts, but to the innocent convention of the pastoral established by such classical poets as Theocritus and Virgil. A special mention might be made of the English pastoral poet William Shenstone, a gardener like Finlay whose image of 'Venus semi-reducta' (the goddess of beauty half concealed in a Virgilian grove) recalls this device of the camouflaged tank. In the original emblem, however, attention was cast not so much upon the pastoral predilections of the Muses themselves, as on the choice of the inspired poet to live in rural solitude. 'Loneliness is appropriate for those who are contemplating some outstanding action', runs a contemporary commentary; 'for how can one sing well in noisy conditions?' The choice of the solitary sparrow (rather than, say, the nightingale) to embody the poet is not an obvious one. Inevitably it recalls biblical, rather than classical prototypes—perhaps the Psalmist's 'sparrow, that sitteth alone upon the house-top'?

The device of the camouflaged tank thus accentuates what already seems implicit in the earlier emblem. Pastoral poetry is not merely idyllic. The image of rural retreat must be accommodated with that of the solitariness of the soul. Venus may be, as Racine in the steps of Euripides reminds us, 'toute entière à sa proie attachée'. And engagement with the Muses may offer its own, lightly camouflaged dangers.

ET IN ARCADIA
EGO

One of Panofsky's most justly celebrated essays in iconology (the term he takes directly from Cesare Ripa) is concerned with Poussin's painting *Et in Arcadia Ego*. Contemporary disputes about the significance of this enigmatic work lead him back to Greek pastoral poetry and the progressive formation of the cultural concept of 'Arcady', with its almost infinite tissue of poetic references converging upon the point that even here, in the ideal pastoral world, death is present. But Panofsky has not checked the speculation about the inner meaning of Poussin's picture, which may indeed be bound up with a hermetic interpretation of the golden section and might even lead (it has been suggested) to the rediscovery of the lost treasure of the Albigensian heretics in a particular part of southwestern France.

The metaphorical presentation of the tank *as* Poussin's inscribed monument, within the Arcadian setting, offers us not so much an emblem as an enigma. Estienne describes the role of Enigma as that of serving 'as a Rind or Bark to conserve all the mysteries of our Ancestors wisdome'. We are not immediately tempted to generalise or extend the implications that we see, as in the 'moral' emblem. The treasure, such as it is, is necessarily remote from us, and we have no foolproof method of lifting the hermetic seal (an oblique comment on the fact that here, particularly, Finlay's adoption of a pre-existent motif has proved a stumbling-block to those who would deny the relevance of wide-ranging cultural reference, Estienne's 'ignoramusses').

[7]

HABITARVNT DI
QVOQVE SILVAS

EVEN GODS HAVE DWELT IN WOODS

The motto is the closing part of a hexameter from Virgil's *Eclogues*, a borrowing which recalls Estienne's precept that quotations from classical poets fall outside the general rule of concision in mottoes (and a normal restriction to three words). We move from the tank, camouflaged or as a monument, to another term of modern warfare: in this case the American heavy cruiser *Minneapolis* is shown in her leafy camouflage, against a woodland setting (the device is based on an actual photograph). The line from Virgil is re-animated by the substitution of new 'Gods' for old, the modern fighting ship for the pagan deities whose manifestation in the sylvan setting might have been taken as equally marvellous, or anomalous, in the classical period.

 Minneapolis seems, in addition, a curiously apt point of reference for this emblem. Not only does it recall, in its apparently Greek etymology, the profusion of cities named with the same suffix ('polis' =city) dotted over Asia in the wake of Alexander's conquests—a fair analogy for America's imperial might. It also suggests a kind of homage to the present-day American artist Charles Biederman, an inhabitant of the woodlands of the state of which Minneapolis is capital, a translator of Cézanne's painting into the terms of the 'structurist relief' and the author of an issue of Finlay's magazine *Poor. Old. Tired. Horse.*, in which his 'Artistic Credo' was illustrated exclusively by photographs of woodland.

In this emblem, the seemingly innocent pun which allows us to shift from 'Paros' to 'Paras' (and from singular to plural) mobilises a whole series of cultural references which are, so to speak, encapsulated in the image. The original motto is a one-line poem by the French poet Emmanuel Lochac, published in the 1930's and doubtless a reflection of the influence of Apollinaire. Yet in its content it is a strong evocation of the Neo-classic tradition, perhaps of Winckelmann's lyrical passages on Graeco-Roman sculpture where the 'eternal action' of the marble and its 'immobility' are equally stressed. The substitution of 'Paras' for 'Paros' (the island specially associated with the production of Greek marble) allows a new, hyperbolic image to supplant the old: the descent of parachutes against the blue sky having the same quality of 'eternal action' as the immobile, classic art. At this point, where the conjunction could clearly have been made by an image of descending parachutes, meaning has been displaced once again through a return to the cherished garden imagery of the emblem books. We have not simply parachutes as classic art, but roses as parachutes as classic art (the supplementary meaning being made possible, of course, by an image which allows the rose-bush to assume this metaphor, as well as by the Spanish custom of calling the parachute the 'rose of death').

Would it be appropriate to suggest yet another displacement? To the poet's own garden, Stonypath, where such a white rose-bush, sedulously trained over its parachute-like frame, will undoubtedly appear one of these days.

COMINVS ET EMINVS

The motto is a well-used one, which refers respectfully to the original purpose of the *impresa*: in Estienne's words, to 'signifie a gallant and heroicke action'. The connotation of 'near and far' is employed to suggest the formidable extent of kingly power in the period of the growth of the nation-state, and as such was a favourite choice of such monarchs as Louis XII of France. The traditional device accompanying the text— the porcupine with its legendary powers of offence through shooting its quills and more credible powers of defence through curling into a ball—is here replaced by that of the self-propelled gun, developed increasingly since the later stages of World War II. Unlike early versions (such as the unfortunate German tank-destroyer 'Elefant'), the American gun depicted has a long-range capacity supplemented by a small gun for close-in protection of both gun and crew.

The simplicity of both motto and device enables them to work on the level of moral instruction. That one should beware of attack from close at hand at the very point of launching one's heavier artillery against the enemy is, after all, a practical and salutary warning. It is in accord with the pervasiveness of the original emblems that the heroic can thus be used to suggest almost a measure of domestic caution. Or perhaps it is the other way round: a reincorporation of domestic caution into an overall strategy of offence.

COMINVS ET EMINVS

'By the way, let us observe with Bargagli, that his ingenuity must not be condemned, who from the same matter (whereof others have made use) seeketh new qualities, which he expresseth in another manner, and applies to new designes' (Estienne).

From moral counsel to a poetic meditation which sets an event of modern warfare against a broad and suggestive cultural context. The scuttling of the German battleship *Graf Spee* off Montevideo in the early part of the Second World War was an event which powerfully impressed the popular imagination throughout the world. When, after a long and solitary cruise, the *Graf Spee* was finally destroyed to avoid capture, the image of the armoured mast-tower sinking against a lurid, tropical sunset provided a graphic emblem of her fate. Contemporary descriptions record the final explosion as producing a cloud of smoke like 'some giant brown stone-pine', a detail which is reproduced in this image and enables the transposition on to an entirely new level of connotation. The *Graf Spee*'s journey to the far south, where the manifestation of the stone pine *in extremis* recalls the fir trees of her northern homeland, is seen against the abiding sense of estrangement ('pining') which characterises Northern culture. In the same way as Kitaj titles his evocation of the Spanish Civil War with the words of Goethe's haunting song, 'Kennst du das Land / Wo die Zitronen blühn' ('Knowst thou the land / Where the Lemon-trees bloom'), so this conflation explores the gap between North and South through dramatising a sense of estrangement, and menace. But in this case, Kitaj's bitter irony is absent. The self-inflicted death at sunset, far from home, has a quality of epic grandeur.

Far from its base, the carrier fighter lies,
  Homeless in water, outcast of the skies.
Icarus thus too far outstretched his span,
  Bringing to nought the artifice of Man.
Though you have wings that melt not in the Sun,
  Seek not to test the limits of your run!

Gombrich takes the original form of this *impresa*, and the 'five closely printed pages' of commentary on it by Ruscelli, as illustrating the fertility of 'free-floating metaphor'. The motto, 'Hence brighter', accompanied by the device of a sun behind clouds, supplies a 'formula' on which we are able to meditate. 'Somehow such an image reveals an aspect of the world which would seem to elude the ordered progress of dialectic argument.' Of course the success of such an *impresa* in provoking meditation and commentary is not simply a function of the compressed and suggestive form of the original. It is crucial that the reference evoked should be to the presence and absence of light. The commentary can therefore draw upon the manifold implications of light as a metaphysical substance, ranging back to such sources as St. Augustine who held that all knowledge was acquired through 'divine illumination of the intellect'. It can draw upon a philosophical tradition which, from Neo-Platonism onwards, has been particularly congenial to the poet.

In this *impresa*, the translation of device is no more than a simple substitution. Instead of the sun behind clouds, we have the image of the Heinkel He-219A Uhu ('Owl') night fighter which first flew in 1942. The 'Owl' in its moonlight camouflage recalls the use of birds in the original emblems, while its protruding aerials denote the presence of radar—a device for obtaining 'brightness' of vision out of darkness. An additional feature is the provision of upward-firing cannons, which were ideally intended to hit intruding bombers on the wings, thereby igniting their fuel tanks and 'illuminating' the night sky.

[19]

> Through that pure virgin-shrine,
> That sacred veil drawn o'er thy glorious noon,
> That men might look and live, as glow-worms shine
>   And face the moon;
>   Wise Nicodemus saw such light
>   As made him know his God by night.

Henry Vaughan's poem, 'The Night', invokes Nicodemus, the wise man who came to seek out Jesus by night in order to learn the secret of salvation. For Vaughan, the night is a 'shrine', in which the mysteries of the true light are veiled from view, and the searcher after truth, who would otherwise be dazzled by its brilliance, has the task of training his own miniature apparatus of perception upon the occluded prospect. That he is able to see in the night is, of course, a result of the fact that God has planted all creation with the 'seeds' of eternal light: even the flint-stone—which gives its title to Vaughan's *Silex Scintillans*—reveals by its flashes of mica the destiny of all sublunary matter to act as a theophany, leading men towards the eternal unclouded being. The radar screen serves in this way as an image of the hermetic pursuit, of the task of the skilled operator who locates the material object beyond normal vision and registers it as pure intelligibility—the moving dot of light upon the opaque screen. But the hermetic pursuit—the destiny of the mystic—involves not only the discipline of proceeding from the visible to the intelligible world. It is also a transformation of the person, a humility beyond wisdom, a darkness beyond brightness—in Vaughan's words:

> There is in God (some say)
> A deep, but dazzling darkness; as men here
> Say it is late and dusky, because they
> See not all clear.
> O for that night! where I in him
> Might live invisible and dim.

The motto is taken from a seventeenth-century Spanish painting entitled *The Knight's Dream*. Jewels, gold, luxurious materials, costly foods—all the vanities of the world are spread out as a 'memento mori' before the sleeping knight, and the solemn warning is intensified by the insertion of an emblem: the image of an arrow against the sun supplemented with the above text. 'It stings eternally, it flies swiftly and it kills'. Problems of interpretation inevitably arise in relation to this emblem. Is the arrow to be taken as an 'arrow of desire', indicating the perpetual force which consumes us as it feeds upon the pleasures of the world? In that case, what of its juxtaposition with the sun? Does the sun represent eternity, and the arrow Time, which 'flies' and finally kills? Would it then be implied that the arrow is a kind of sun-beam, a materialisation of the sun's light which carries its burning, consuming qualities into our bodies? If so, this would be almost a reversal of the light metaphysic, and the spiritual motif of 'turning towards the light'.

The image of the modern jet-fighter against the sun accentuates this clash with the metaphysical theme. The plane is more deadly when it attacks 'out of the sun', it flies more swiftly than an arrow and its sting delivered through wing missiles might well be the killing flame of napalm. The hyperbole, which takes us to the verge of the unspeakable, at the same time renews the insidious charge of the original emblem.

Estienne's treatise cites the authority of Contile for the view that mottoes should be taken from the 'Spanish tongue above all others for love matters'. This would ratify the present usage of this motto, 'To None Other', which is taken as an indication of the fatal power of romantic love. An original emblem exists in which the same motto, devised by Don Garzia di Toledo, accompanies the device of the mariner's needle 'which, as if gifted with eyesight, turns by itself to the lodestar'. The new image plays equally on the concept of the 'wonderful', the device which appears to overstep 'the ordinary laws of Nature'. But it adds the warning of ultimate destruction. The missile homes in upon the fated plane, attracted by the heat of its engine, and speeds towards the consummation that will destroy them both.

The codes of romantic love supply innumerable examples of the common fate which awaits star-crossed lovers. But the example which is perhaps most acutely akin to the modern image presented here is that offered by Goethe's novel *The Elective Affinities*. Goethe also explores the metaphor supplied by contemporary scientific research: the 'fatal' attraction between men and women already wedded to other partners is placed on a level of chemical inevitability. It should be added however that Goethe's plot (delightfully reassumed in Truffaut's film *Jules et Jim*) explores the gap between the bio-chemical and the social determinants without offering any definitive conclusion. Here the issue is unequivocal.

Like the 'Thunderbolt' motto, this is in origin a pre-Socratic fragment. Its author, Empedokles, may have intended an explicitly sexual reference, as to the 'cleft' meadows of the 'Mons Veneris'. But the adjective could as well be taken as 'divided', an interpretation which here lends itself both to the 'divided meadow' of the aircraft carrier's flight deck, and to the sea itself, split between warring fleets (the Greek word for 'divided' is the one from which we take the term 'schism'). Just as Empedokles sought to embody the cosmological categories of Love and Strife in the mythological guise of the Olympian deities, so the carrier suggests a contemporary equivalent in our own culture for the ultimate ideas of power and beauty. But it is an identification which passes through, and is enriched by, the element of 'Pagan Mystery' in the art and literature of the Renaissance—the Renaissance which shows us Aphrodite rising newborn from the waves with her attendant Zephyrs.

:FITTING THESE TOGETHER WITH RIVETS OF LOVE: APHRODITE·

The structure is once again composed of three levels of interconnected reference. The 'motto', or fragment from Empedokles, supplies the initial datum: a form of language in which poetry, mythology and philosophy are not discriminated one from another, and the short verbal formula—probably rescued as a quotation from the margin of some later text—remains perpetually open and inexhaustible in its implications. The Renaissance gives us a richer and more definite content, conveyed in the celebrated pictures of 'Mars and Venus' which Botticelli, Veronese and many other painters left behind them. The modern reference makes a new identification necessary—incites us to a new distribution of the related roles. Aphrodite is perhaps to be identified with her place of birth the sea; Mars, her seducer in the Renaissance pictures, rides upon her as aircraft carrier upon the waves. The dipping and soaring of the small planes suggests the attendant Cupids, or in Edgar Wind's terms 'infant satyrs', that attend the spectacle of adultery among the Gods.

Both these mottoes from Empedokles pose a problem beyond the identification and the extended metaphor. When we return, as it were, to this undifferentiated state of language, this poetic cosmology revived in our own time in the philosophy of Heidegger, we are not simply paying homage to an outworn idiom. If Aphrodite (Venus) borrows the tools of her husband, the blacksmith Hephaistos (Vulcan), what will she fit together with her rivets? Surely the chains of language itself, weighted and worked by desire.

The U.S.S. *Enterprise* appears by name as the final, evolved exemplar of the modern warship. It also unites in itself the different elements of the cosmology of Heraclitus: earth being represented in the landing ground offered by the carrier deck, air by the element in which its aircraft move, fire by the dynamic and destructive character of its nuclear capacity and water by the surrounding ocean. Modern physics has set up a progressively more accurate picture of the material world which is analogous in imaginative terms to the world of the pre-Socratics. In the same way, the nuclear-powered carrier embodies in intimate and terrifying conjunction the power released by the splitting of the atom, and the poetic message of union of the elements.

One may well wish to meditate further upon the purpose of this invocation of Heraclitean cosmology in relation to modern nuclear warfare. It is as if this vicarious presence in the age which immediately preceded the establishment of the Western aesthetic codex, with Plato, were a method of gaining priority over the Platonic system. As if, on the other hand, the references to the modern fighting fleet were intended to bracket off the codes of warfare—the epic, the chivalric and indeed the romantic view of sea-faring being radically foreclosed in the elemental heroism of the nuclear confrontation. In a sense, the operation of these two brackets (the first anticipating Platonic and Aristotelian aesthetics, and the second demarcating the codes of the past) places the Western cultural tradition in parenthesis. And the self-contained form of the medallion seems to be the precise correlative to this poetic act.

Like the previous one, this emblem uses a motto in the form of a one-word poem, the original title being 'Kleiner Kreuzer Sonata' and the one-word text 'Emden'. An analogy is established between the 'Kleiner Kreuzer' (Light Cruiser) *Emden* and the well-known 'Kreu[t]zer Sonata' for Violin and Piano by Beethoven. It is as if the classic status of the musical composition, well attested by countless performances, were also being claimed for the exploits of the German warship, which became a legend for its lonely forays against Allied shipping in the Indian Ocean at the outset of the First World War (and was the subsequent inspiration for the fated journey of the *Graf Spee*).

Once again we respond to what Frank Kermode calls 'a modern way with the classic'. Captain von Müller's achievement has been compared with that of the French raiders in old sea-faring days. His lightning descents upon merchant shipping inevitably recall the more or less piratical exploits of the English sea captains in the wars with France and Spain. But it must be recognised that his task was precisely to manage the 'detached ship' in modern conditions. The connotations of virtuosity implicit in the comparison enable us to extend its imaginative dimensions. Beethoven's Sonata takes its name from the virtuoso to whom it was dedicated. Perhaps the elaborately devious course of the *Emden*, in the interval between its detachment from Admiral von Spee's squadron and its final sinking, can be seen as an unaccompanied cadenza for the virtuoso soloist.

[33]

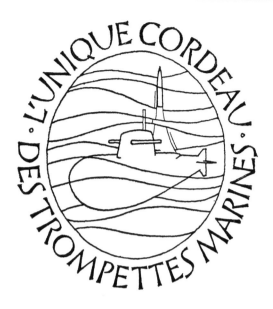

Music also supplies the area of reference for this motto, which is in origin a one-line poem by Guillaume Apollinaire (and may well have been a fragment copied out on the proofs of *Alcools* in 1912). The line acquires its subtlety and attraction from the ambiguity which resides in the two combined phrases. The 'trompette marine' (literally a 'marine trumpet') is in fact a form of stringed instrument: 'l'unique cordeau'—the single string—can also be interpreted as 'l'unique cor d'eau'—the single horn of water (and so back to the imaginary trumpet). Out of this circle of interlocking implications, the French critic André Rouveyre has drawn a wide-ranging commentary extending to some fifteen pages. He refers to 'trumpets rushing like geysers of flame from the watery depths, moving and screaming their heroic salvos with the onslaught of the princely star'. Clearly the plangent line from Apollinaire has become, for Rouveyre, an evocation of the Last Trump, the Apocalypse, in which the sea gives up its dead and the book of life is opened. In this emblem, the hyperbolic interpretation is adopted and converted. The apocalyptic message of the deep is the nuclear missile.

Rouveyre's fifteen pages, like Ruscelli's 'five closely printed' ones, raise the question of the *economy* of the commentary. What is appropriate to the original point of departure? Is there a measure which might offend the Delphic inscription 'nothing too much'? Only, one supposes, if the commentary is conceived as distinct from the 'work' (the emblem). But if the emblem itself is seen, in its divided and united body and soul, as a meeting place of texts, a tissue of traditions, then the commentary is simply a further stage in the spinning of this tissue. There is no economy of the essential and the inessential which could govern this process.

OUT OF THE STRONG CAME FORTH SWEETNESS

An argument about the persistence of the emblem in everyday usage might well take as its example the trademark of Tate & Lyle, who use the motto above in combination with the image of a dead lion on their tins of syrup. The original reference is to the story of Samson in the Book of Judges, and relates to a riddle which the strong man is obliged to solve. The verbal formula is explained by reference to a lion's carcase, in which the bees have started to make honey. Here the terms of the reference are altered to include H.M.S. *Lion*, one of the largest of British warships, and the helicopters which swarm like bees above her improvised helicopter deck. The contrast obtained in the original between strength and sweetness works on this new level, but in an unexpected way. Not only does the warship provision the helicopters, storing their (honey) fuel for them. But it may be called upon to contradict its usual warlike role and supply relief in times of famine and flood: in this case the stored 'honey' is of the most direct benefit.

As with the 'Semper festina lente' emblem, this works through a kind of oxymoron—the juxtaposition of opposed terms. But here the terms are slightly displaced: the direct antitheses would be strong/weak, sour/sweet, and the conjunction strong/sweet plays on the vestigial sense that the other terms have been suppressed. The figure used in the motto is a synecdoche, 'sweetness' being conceived as a 'part' of the 'whole' which is strength. But there is also the metonymic substitution of 'sweetness' for 'bees' (the contained for the container), which parallels on the verbal level the visual antithesis between the one and the

[37]

many (ship/lion and helicopters/bees). The apparent simplicity of the emblem therefore belies a complex rhetorical structure: this is the under-pinning which allows the immediate message to be retained as a text for meditation.

In this emblem, the conventional language of aerial warfare is transformed by association, the various terms reverting to their original sense. 'Contrails'—the vapour trails left by a plane at high altitudes—bring with them the connotation of 'angel', which is a term used by pilots to signify a unit of height. 'Bandit' was the code name for intruding German aircraft during the Battle of Britain. The final term, 'Saints', does not possess such alternative meanings: it is used to restore the primary meanings of the two previous terms, and impels us to make a yet further supplementary identification—the oval vapour trail as the plane's 'halo'.

Paul Nash commemorated the Battle of Britain with a picture of vapour trails over the Thames Estuary. Finlay also isolates the soaring plane in its tracks and makes it a symbol of spiritual struggle, lending an additional dimension through the antithesis between 'bandits' and 'angels/saints' which leads us to think of the Crucifixion (Christ between two robbers). Although contemporary allusions are employed, the direction given to our thoughts is the same as when Hooker breaks off his political discussions to contemplate the existence of angels: 'we may lift up our eyes (as it were) from the footstool to the throne of God'.

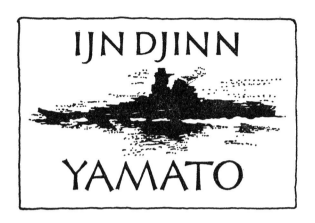

IJN DJINN YAMATO

The series of four emblems which closes the collection takes as its point of reference the Pacific War between the United States and Japan. The *Yamato*, at the time the world's largest battleship and a remarkable tour de force of construction, was designed to dominate the Ocean with its presence. It finally succumbed to American attack only as late as April 1945. 'IJN'—the contracted form of 'Imperial Japanese Navy'—is here used to summon up an unexpected connotation: that of the 'Djinn' or 'Djinnie' raised by the rubbing of Aladdin's Lamp. The *Yamato* is seen as an equally powerful and magical manifestation of the small (lamp-shaped?) islands of Japan.

The form of the emblem is not simply a means of sketching out an extended metaphor. Here, as in almost every case, reference is made to a specific cultural code, which is both cited and placed in suspension. Aladdin and the stories of the *Thousand and One Nights* are the very archetype of story-telling; they weave a continuous web of fiction in which the fantastic is a constant resource to be drawn upon. By contrast, the magic of the *Yamato* is short-lived, and the story within which it makes its appearance stops brutally short just after its own demise.

The Battle of Midway was fought between the fleets of the United States and Japan in June 1942. The Japanese strategists had long been preparing for a 'decisive fleet action' in the Pacific, and the Commander in Chief of the Japanese fleet rightly calculated that a threat to Midway Island—the westernmost outpost of the Hawaiian island chain—would compel the Americans to engage their comparatively weaker forces. In effect, the battle was finally decided in America's favour, and marked the turning point both of the War in the Pacific and, arguably, the entire World War.

The motto of this emblem complements the 'Midway' theme with the celebrated opening lines of Dante's *Divine Comedy*: 'In the middle of the journey of our life ['Midway'], I came to myself in a dark wood'. The 'dark wood' of Dante's allegory is recreated in the image of bursts of anti-aircraft fire, which can be seen covering the sky in surviving photographs of the battle. Just as Dante has embodied the complexity of middle age in his image of the 'dark wood', so the emblem suggests a predicament of choice. The 'turning point' is also, perhaps, the mystic's 'dark night of the soul', with the promise of a successful outcome no more assured for one fleet than for the other.

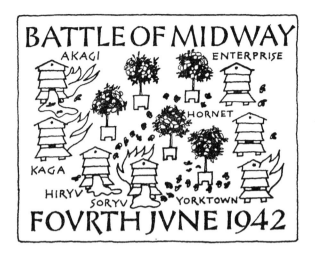

BATTLE OF MIDWAY
AKAGI   ENTERPRISE
HORNET
KAGA
HIRYV
SORYV   YORKTOWN
FOVRTH JVNE 1942

If the previous emblem takes as its motif the entry into the 'dark wood' of battle, this one celebrates the crucial events that were to determine its outcome. Under the emblematic cover of a Renaissance pastoral, we see enacted the conflict of 4 June 1942, when the four ships of Admiral Naguno's I Carrier Striking Force were destroyed by dive-bombers from their American counterparts, *Enterprise* and *Hornet* (*Yorktown* being the major American casualty). The dramatic success of this action depended on the fact that the American planes were able to engage the Japanese fleet at its most vulnerable—whilst each of the carriers bore a full deckload of armed and fuelled aircraft. The effect of American bombing was therefore to ignite petrol tanks, bombs and torpedoes, causing unquenchable conflagration. The analogy of the Renaissance garden shows us the carriers as hives, the American attack planes as swarming bees and the conflagration of overspilling honey. Formal trees in tubs fill out the pastoral conception, while signifying at the same time the ocean, in whose lush distances the opposing carriers were concealed from each other.

At Stonypath, Ian Hamilton Finlay's home in Lanarkshire, there is an interaction and interpenetration of the Garden and the Ocean. A series of stretches of water of greater and less magnitude is juxtaposed with the enclosed (the 'inland') garden. But even within the garden, poem inscriptions pick up the distant murmur of the sea. The axis of this opposition, which can hardly be explained more fully in this context, has perhaps become the base structure of Finlay's poetics.

BATTLE OF MIDWAY
FOVRTH JVNE 1942

HIC PERIERVNT
AKAGI·KAGA·SORYV
HIRYV·YORKTOWN
ÆQVORIS·ALVI·MEL·SV-
VM·FLAMMIFERVM·EA
CONSVMPSIT·VNACVM
EXAMINIBVS·OPTIMIS

HERE PERISHED
AKAGI KAGA SORYU HIRYU
YORKTOWN THE SEA-HIVES
CONSUMED WITH THEIR MOST
CHOICE SWARMS BY THEIR
OWN FLAME-BEARING HONEY

The emblem has a distant, but crucial kinship with the inscription. Indeed at a certain point, the tradition of the emblem appears almost to fuse with that of epigraphy, the medallion forming the essential link between the two. In Plutarch's dialogue 'Concerning the E at Delphi', the hypothesis is brought forward of an inscription (consisting of one letter) whose immemorial origin both resists secure interpretation and provokes the most fruitful commentary. Perhaps it is appropriate that the succession of hermetic and ingenious readings should terminate eventually at the most impersonal and pure: the E as 'thou art', a simple evocation of Apollo as pure being. Perhaps it is also appropriate that this collection should end with a memorial inscription. The register of evocations comes to a close in the laconic classical form, and in the permanence of stone.

BIBLIOGRAPHY

INTRODUCTION

Mario Praz: *Studies in Seventeenth-Century Imagery*, Second Edition, Rome, 1964.

R. J. Clements: *Picta Poesis: Literary and Humanistic Theory in Renaissance Emblem Books*, Rome, 1960.

Arthur Henkel and Albrecht Schöne (eds.): *Emblemata, Handbuch zur Sinnbildkunst des XVI. und XVII. Jahrhunderts*, Stuttgart, 1967.

Cesare Ripa: 'Introduction à l'Iconologie' (French trans. with introd. by Hubert Damisch), in *Critique*, August–September 1973.

E. H. Gombrich: *Symbolic Images*, London, 1972.

John Bunyan: *Divine Emblems* (originally *A Book for Boys and Girls; or, Country Rhimes for Children*), 1686.

R. L. Stevenson: *Moral Emblems*, Davos-Platz, 1882.

Henry Estienne: *The Art of Making Devises* (trans. Thomas Blount), London, 1652.

Harold Bloom: *A Map of Misreading*, New York, 1975.

THUNDERBOLT STEERS ALL

G. S. Kirk (ed.), *Heraclitus—The Cosmic Fragments*; Burnet, *Early Greek Philosophy*; Walter Pater, *Plato and Platonism*; Karl Jaspers, *The Great Philosophers*, Vol. II; Robert J. Icks, *Famous Tank Battles*; Richard M. Ogorkiewicz, *Armoured Forces*; Chamberlain and Ellis, *Tanks of the World 1914–45*; General Heinz Guderian, *Panzer Leader*.

SEMPER FESTINA LENTE

Praz, *Studies in Seventeenth-Century Imagery*; Kenneth Macksey, *The Guinness Book of Tank Facts & Feats*; R. J. Clements, *Picta Poesis*; Aesop, *Fables*.

WOODLAND IS PLEASING TO THE MUSES

Psalm 102; William Shenstone, *Works*; Dr Johnson, *Lives of the Poets*; Major General F. W. von Mellenthin, *Panzer Battles*; William Cowper, *Letters*; Lieut-Colonel C. H. R. Chesney D.S.O., *The Art of Camouflage*; David Gascoyne, *Hölderlin's Madness*; Martin Heidegger, *Hölderlin and the Essence of Poetry*.

ET IN ARCADIA EGO

Virgil, *Eclogues*; John Sparrow, *Visible Words*; E. Panofsky, *Meaning in the Visual Arts*; Walter Friedlaender, *Nicolas Poussin*; Elizabeth Wheeler Manwaring, *Italian Landscape in Eighteenth Century England*; F. M. von Senger und Etterlin, *Die deutschen Panzer 1926–45*; *Wenn alle Brüder Schweigen* (foreword by Colonel-General Paul Hausser).

HABITARUNT DI QUOQUE SILVAS

Virgil, *Eclogues*; Plutarch, *Isis and Osiris*; Proclus, *The Elements of Theology*; *Encyclopedia of Sea Warfare*; Silverstone, *U.S. Warships of World War II*; Charles Biederman, *Art as the Evolution of Visual Knowledge*.

ÉTERNELLE ACTION DU PAROS IMMOBILE · ÉTERNELLE ACTION DES PARAS IMMOBILES

Emmanuel Lochac, *Monostiches*; Winckelmann, *Von der Nachahmung der griechischen Werke in der Malerei und Bildhauerkunst*; Charles Whiting, *Hunters From the Sky*; Graham Stuart Thomas, *Climbing Roses Old and New*.

COMINUS ET EMINUS (1)

Praz, *Studies in Seventeenth-Century Imagery*; Henry Estienne, *The Art of Making Devises*; Giovio, *Dialogo delle Imprese* (cit. Praz); F. M. von Senger und Etterlin, *Taschenbuch der Panzer*; John Batchelor and Ian Hogg, *Artillery*; Geoffrey Jukes, *Kursk, the Clash of Armour*.

COMINUS ET EMINUS (2)

Sir Eugen Millington-Drake, *The Drama of Graf Spee and The Battle of The Plate*; Kapitän zür See Gerhard Bidlingmaier (ret'd), *KM Admiral Graf Spee*; W. J. Stokoe, *The Observers' Book of Trees*; William Vaughan, Helmut Börsch-Supan and Hans Joachim Neidhardt, *Caspar David Friedrich*.

COMINUS ET EMINUS (3)

Mitsuo Fuchida and Masatake Okumiya, *Midway*; Richard M. Bueschel, *Mitsubishi A6M1/2/ – 2N*; Ovid, *Metamorphoses*; A. J. Barker, *Midway, the Turning Point*.

HINC CLARIOR (2)

Plotinus, *The Enneads*; Kathleen Raine and George Mills Harper, *Thomas Taylor the Platonist*; Henry Vaughan, *Silex Scintillans*; E. H. Gombrich, *Symbolic Images*; Alfred Price, *Instruments of Darkness*; William Green, *Warplanes of the Third Reich*; C. F. Rawnsley and Robert Wright, *Night Fighter*.

AETERNE PUNGT CITO VOLAT ET OCCIDIT

Letters of Marsilio Ficino (preface by Paul Oskar Kristeller); *Encyclopedia of Air Warfare*.

A NIUN' ALTRA

Praz, *Studies in Seventeenth-Century Imagery*; *Encyclopedia of Air Warfare*; Goethe, *The Elective Affinities*.

THE DIVIDED MEADOWS OF APHRODITE

Burnet, *Early Greek Philosophy*; Kirk and Raven, *The Presocratic Philosophers*; Werner Jaeger, *The Theology of the Early Greek Philosophers*; Edgar Wind, *Pagan Mysteries of the Renaissance*; Donald Macintyre, *Aircraft Carrier—The Majestic Weapon*.

APHRODITE FITTING THESE TOGETHER WITH RIVETS OF LOVE

The Hymns of Orpheus; Plotinus, *The Enneads*; Burnet, *Early Greek Philosophy*; Edgar Wind, *Pagan Mysteries in the Renaissance*; Geoffrey Grigson, *The Goddess of Love*; Donald Macintyre, *Aircraft Carrier—The Majestic Weapon*.

A CELEBRATION OF EARTH, AIR, FIRE, WATER

Furley and Allen (eds.), *Studies in Presocratic Philosophy*, Vol. 1; Plato, *Timaeus*; R. D. Hicks, *Stoic & Epicurean*; Sandbach, *The Stoics*; Edward Hussey, *The Presocratics*; G. S. Kirk and J. E. Raven, *The Presocratic Philosophers*; F. Nietzsche, *The Birth of Tragedy*; Simone Weil, *Gateway to God*; Gareth L. Pawlowski, *Flat-Tops and Fledglings*; Commander W. H. Cracknell, *USS Enterprise (CVAN 65)*.

THE LAST CRUISE OF THE EMDEN

Cicero, *The Offices*; Keith Middlemas, *Command the Far Seas*; Edwin P. Hoyt, *The Last Cruise of the Emden*; Rear-Admiral Alfred T. Mahan, *On Naval Warfare*; Richard Haugh, *The Pursuit of Admiral von Spee*.

L'UNIQUE CORDEAU DES TROMPETTES MARINES
The Revelation of St. John the Divine; G. Apollinaire, *Alcools*; André
Rouveyre, *Amour et poésie d'Apollinaire* (quoted in *Roy Rogers*, Winter
1974); Michel Décaudin, *Le Dossier d'Alcools*; Commander Nicholas
Whitestone, *The Submarine: The Ultimate Weapon.*

OUT OF THE STRONG CAME FORTH SWEETNESS
Judges 14; W. G. D. Blundell, *Ships of the Modern Royal Navy.*

ANGELS, BANDITS, SAINTS
Luke 23; Richard Hooker, *Of the Laws of Ecclesiastical Polity*; Marcel
Jullian, *The Battle of Britain*; H. St. George Saunders, *The Battle of Brit-
ain*; Alfred Price, *World War II Fighter Conflict*; Adolf Galland, *The
First and the Last*; William Green, *Augsburg Eagle*; Robert Wright,
Dowding and the Battle of Britain; Field-Marshal von Kesselring, *Mem-
oirs*; John Vader, *Spitfire.*

IJN DJINN
The Thousand and One Nights; Masataka Chihaya, *IJN Yamato*; *The
Japanese Navy in World War II* (introd. Dr. Raymond O'Connor);
Andrieu D'Albas, *Death of a Navy.*

THROUGH A DARK WOOD
Dante, *The Divine Comedy*; Mitsuo Fuchida and Masatake Okumiya,
Midway; Samuel Eliot Morison, *History of United States Naval Opera-
tions in World War II*, Vol. IV; A. J. Barker, *Midway, the Turning Point.*

BATTLE OF MIDWAY—FOURTH JUNE 1942 (1)
Virgil, *Georgics*; Mitsuo Fuchida and Masatake Okumiya, *Midway*;
Samuel Eliot Morison, *History of United States Naval Operations in
World War II*, Vol. IV; Derek Clifford, *A History of Garden Design*;
Barbara Jones, *Follies and Grottoes*; Julia S. Berrall, *The Garden*; Sir
Christopher Andrewes, *The Lives of Bees and Wasps.*

BATTLE OF MIDWAY—FOURTH JUNE 1942 (2)
Plutarch, *The E at Delphi.*

PRINTED AT THE STINEHOUR PRESS,
LUNENBURG, VERMONT, IN AN EDITION OF 750 COPIES,
OF WHICH 26 ARE NUMBERED AND SIGNED